jazz portraits an eye for the sound

jazz portraits an eye for the sound

images of jazz and jazz musicians

tim motion

foreword by ronnie scott

SMITHMARK

a salamander book

This edition published in 1995 by SMITHMARK Publishers Inc., 16 East 32nd Street, New York, NY 10016

9 8 7 6 5 4 3 2

SMITHMARK books are available for bulk purchase for sales promotion and premium use. For details write or call the manager of special sales, SMITHMARK Publishers Inc., 16 East 32nd Street, New York, NY 10016; (212) 532-6600

ISBN 0-8317-1023-3

All correspondence concerning the content of this book should be addressed to Salamander Books Ltd , 129–137 York Way, London N7 9LG, England

CREDITS
Editor: Richard Collins
Designer: Paul Johnson
Color reproduction and printing by CS Graphics PTE Ltd, Singapore
Printed in Singapore

Charlie 'Bird' Parker

Painting by Tim Motion

contents

Thelonious

slates fall
as if hap
hazardly
from the house
you build
so carefully
of scales -

just so   sky high
you don't need to fly

and no more blue
than pleases you

Michael Horovitz

foreword

The attraction that jazz musicians have for photographers is understandable when one considers that both are concerned with *the moment.* For the musician it is the fleeting moment that involves the creation of some kind of valid music and for the photographer the attempt to express it in pictorial terms. And if it isn't concerned with the musician actually in action there is something about the faces and attitudes of jazz musicians that is somehow special.

This affinity seems confined specifically to jazz music – most portraits of classical musicians could just as well be of politicians or bank managers and it seems to be mandatory that photographs of rock musicians consist almost entirely of sullen youths displaying various degrees of misery, acne and teenage angst.

I remember as a young musician avidly collecting those marvellous publicity stills of bands like Tommy Dorsey, Harry James, Teddy Powell, Artie Shaw – full of shiny instruments and young men in sharp suits. The art of jazz photography has sinced progressed toward deeply evocative and perceptive pictures of the faces of those men and women who have spent their lives making spontaneous music. Photographers like Francis Wolff, Bill Claxton, Bill Gottlieb and Herman Leonard from America, Jean-Pierre Leloir from France and Giuseppe Pino from Italy, and from England Tim Motion, David Redfern and Val Wilmer have all demonstrated an enormous sympathy and understanding for jazz musicians.

Tim Motion has compiled an eclectic selection of superb images. I'm not going to single out specific photographs from this collection – they all have something to say. I suggest you look at the pictures, and somehow by some mysterious process, you will hear the music.

Ronnie Scott

introduction

As a photographer and musician there has always been for me a close relationship between the aural and the visual, and thus a natural progression to photographing jazz musicians. My initiation took place at the Cascais Jazz Festival near Lisbon, Portugal in 1971, an extension of my reportage work with a 1943 Leica and my subscription to *Downbeat*, the American jazz magazine. On stage were the Giants of Jazz, the great names in the major evolutionary phase of jazz music: Dizzy Gillespie, Miles Davis, Sonny Stitt, Dexter Gordon, Thelonious Monk, Art Blakey, Kai Winding, Al McKibbon, Ornette Coleman and Joe Turner. It was an exciting episode that lacked only the physical presence of Lester Young, Charlie Parker, Coleman Hawkins and Bud Powell.

Most of the above musicians feature in this book, although I did not request specific names or period images from the twenty-three photographers concerned. Their initial choice, a difficult one I know, was entirely personal and free from the usual constraints of commercial requirement. It is clear that all are driven by a passion for jazz and jazz musicians, some even suggesting that their photography is a substitute for not being able to play an instrument well enough! However, the title of this book crystallizes the idea of attempting to visualize the sound, seize the fleeting moment, or as Andrew Pothecary puts it, "I want to get something that holds something of the music – is musical itself", a sentiment echoed by several contributing photographers. Val Wilmer, in the introduction to her exhibition "Jazz – Roots and Branches" takes the idea further and expresses it neatly: "Originally my photographs started as decoration for my journalism but they developed into my major weapon for telling the truth. It's not enough to point the camera and take a picture. You've got to get inside that moment – to interpret it, to find more."

Jazz music, the musicians and the jazz life, have been amply documented since the late nineteenth century with photographs and the written word and, although I have great respect for the latter, the image is often diminished surrounded by text; the photograph illustrates the word and the word explains the photograph. Can the image not speak for itself? With the answer to that question in mind I planned this book, not as a comprehensive guide or encyclopaedic record of jazz history, but as a collective appreciation of jazz and jazz musicians through the eye of the photographer, with an obsessive regard for the telling moment, an eye for the sound, and sometimes the silence.

My final selection of photographs including my own work was subjective, and not without an element of serendipity. However, from the mid-forties photographs by Bill Gottlieb, Herman Leonard in the fifties and sixties to Daniel Ferri and Jonathan Oppong-Wiafe in the 1990s, I believe that these images communicate the eloquence of the musicians concerned, sometimes in a more contemplative but nonetheless revealing way.

Tim Motion
London, England, 1995

the photographers

Andrew Pothecary

Jak Kilby

Carolina Benshemesh

Jennifer Sebley

Jean-Pierre Leloir

Francine Winham

Peter Symes

William Gottlieb

Daniel Ferri

Terry Cryer

Jonathan Oppong-Wiafe

Chris Windsor

Bob Willoughby

Bob Douglas

Christian Him

David Redfern

Mephisto

David Sinclair

Tim Motion

Val Wilmer

Ray Avery

Herman Leonard

**Jimmy McGriff, not playing his
Hammond B3, Jazz Café, 1992**

"Once you're into playing jazz there's bugger
all you can do about it, you're helpless; and of
course it's economically disastrous..."

Jim Mullen, *jazz guitarist*

Lee Konitz
London, 1987

"Jazz is like a cockroach – it'll always be there. You can't kill it, because it's a vocation for the people who play it."

Dave O'Higgins, jazz saxophonist

Duke Ellington, the incomparable giant of twentieth-century music, with fans at the Greystone Ballroom, Detroit, 1947

"Stan Kenton can stand in front of a thousand fiddles and a thousand brass and make a dramatic gesture and every studio arranger can nod his head and say, 'Oh, yes, that's done like this.' But Duke merely lifts his finger, three horns make a sound, and I don't know what it is!"

André Previn

DON'T OPEN WINDOWS

© William Gottlieb

Big Sid Catlett, rehearsal rooms, New York, 1947

"A powerful player with extraordinary flexibility, he seemed at ease in all kinds of jazz company, including Louis Armstrong, Benny Goodman, Fletcher Henderson and Charlie Parker."

Brian Case / Stan Britt

© William Gottlieb

Bunk Johnson, New York, 1947

"Bunk was a very sophisticated person. He was at home anyplace and with anybody. He didn't see himself as an antique. He was a contemporary person and wanted to play contemporary music."

Harold Drob

© William Gottlieb

Art Tatum, Rochester, New York, 1946

"...we played two tunes before we cut him loose. Fats was playin' pool and Fletcher and them was playin' cards. All of a sudden, boom, we all dropped out and let Art go. Boy, you could hear a rat piss on cotton! That sumbitch tore that Rhythm Club up! I laugh at these cats that say, 'Well, I finally got a decent piano'. He played *any* of those pianos: he'd play it if it only had four keys on it!"

Roy Eldridge

at the Rhythm Club, Harlem

**Stan Kenton, on tour,
Virginia, 1948**

Lady Day (Billie Holiday) with her dog 'Mister', backstage at The Three Deuces, 52nd Street, New York, 1948

Prez (Lester Young), Detroit, 1946

"Criticized for playing too much like Lester, Brew Moore was emphatic in his response: 'Anybody who *doesn't* play like Prez is *wrong!*' "
Bill Crow

**Bird (Charlie Parker),
Riverside, California, 1953,
with his Grafton saxophone,
sold in 1994 for £93,000...**

"Bird is not dead; he's hiding out somewhere, and will be back with some new shit that will scare everybody to death."

Charles Mingus

In the 1890s, Adolphe Sax had some difficulty getting his invention accepted. This is from a turn of the century instrument review:

"The saxophone is a long instrument bent at both ends. It is alleged to be musical. The creature has a series of tiny taps stuck upon it; when touched they cause the instrument to utter sounds suggesting untold agony."

© Bob Douglas

**Dexter Gordon, Club Oasis,
Los Angeles, 1950**

Dexter says of those exciting days on The Street (52nd Street) New York, 1945: "We just took the music downtown. I still don't believe it. Did it really happen? Was it real? Every day was so... enchanting. I don't think anybody realised how historical the whole period was."

Pete Hamill

Billie Holiday, 1952

"Big Sid Catlett took me under his wing and showed me how to use my brushes so that I could play for Billie Holiday. He was so smooth. I worshipped him. I recall the time when Billie would come on. Like, the tables wouldn't be over, I guess, like sixteen inches around, you know, and they would turn off all the air conditioning, they wouldn't serve anything, the waitresses wouldn't take any orders, everything came to a standstill. And she would come on and just be Billie. It was just that she was the queen.
It was such a beautiful thing."

Roy Battle

© William Gottlieb

Slam Stewart, 52nd Street, 1947

"It was quite an experience, I must say, playing with Art Tatum, he was so great."

(quote to W. Royal Stokes)

© William Gottlieb

Dizzy Gillespie, Detroit, 1947

"It was only a matter of evolution," Dizzy summed up. "That is the story of our music. It evolves and each age has its heroes. So I was the hero of the '40s, then somebody else would come for the '50s, another one for the '60s. But the music of the '40s, the music of Charlie Parker and me, laid a foundation for all of the music that is being played now. So I feel very fine about that, you know, that you've been an influence for musicians to go further."

(quote to W. Royal Stokes)

© Bob Douglas

**Charlie Parker and Max Roach,
Watkins Hotel, Los Angeles, 1953**

© Bob Willoughby

**Billie Holiday at the Tiffany Club,
Los Angeles, 1952**

Cab Calloway in zoot suit and chain, Paramount Theater, New York, 1947

Although not highly rated as a jazz musician himself, he was a fine entertainer, and hired many of the best musicians for his bands.

Duke Ellington and Gene Norman at the Just Jazz Concert, Shrine Auditorium, Los Angeles, 1953

© Bob Willoughby

Gerry Mulligan, recording studios, Los Angeles, 1953

© Bob Willoughby

Chet Baker, Los Angeles, 1953

"The normally 'cool' musicians in the recording studio applauded at the end of Chet's 'take' of My Funny Valentine."

Bob Willoughby

"The most talented trumpet player I ever played with. There was a direct line from his musical ideas to his trumpet."

Gerry Mulligan

© Ray Avery

Shelley Manne, Stars of Jazz TV

Show, Los Angeles, 1956

Shelley Manne gave an interviewer his definition of jazz musicians: "We never play anything the same way once."

Bill Crow

© Ray Avery

Art Pepper, Stars Of Jazz TV

Show, Los Angeles, 1958

Eric Dolphy, Club St. Germain,

Paris, 1959

"At home I used to play, and the birds always used to whistle with me. I would stop what I was working on and play with the birds."

Eric Dolphy

© Mephisto

Sonny Rollins, Club St. Germain, Paris, 1959

"This is my philosophy of playing. It could be 'Mary Had A Little Lamb.' The development of themes, this is the way I play. I don't care what it is, it's what you do with it."

Sonny Rollins

© Terry Cryer

© Terry Cryer

Ray Nance, Bradford, England, 1958

**Henry "Red" Allen and Kid Ory,
England, 1959**

... of Ray Nance on violin: "He swings so
much you wanna kick your momma!"

(quote overheard)

"The Kid from Redbank" William
"Count" Basie, London, 1959

"The Basie Band was twice as powerful as any other band I ever heard; all his musicians seemed to have this 'big' sound. Also, he loved listening to the band, without playing too much himself."

(quote: Ronnie Scott, in conversation)

"My piano? Well, I don't want to run it in the ground, as they say. I love to play, but this idea of one man taking one chorus after another is not wise, in my opinion. Therefore, I feed dancers my own piano in short doses, and when I come in for a solo, I do it unexpectedly, using a strong rhythm background behind me. That way, we figure, the Count's piano isn't going to become monotonous."

Count Basie

Talking of pianos reminds me of the many horror stories relating to the unplayable condition (except to Art Tatum, of course) of many of those instruments encountered on tour in concert halls and clubs. This actually happened to me, in London; I was to play a gig at a wine bar in Baker Street with a pianist friend, the late Jack Hobbs. The bar was in the basement, all black with piped music, and the manager strolled about with a guitar under his arm. Jack was sitting with a large Scotch in his hand staring gloomily at the bright scarlet upright piano. I set up the bass and asked him to give me a "G". He touched the keyboard, and groaned, "Which one do you want?" We complained; the manager glanced nonchalantly at the piano as if it was a houseplant and said, "What's wrong? We had it painted yesterday." It's the truth.

Tim Motion

© Terry Cryer

**Johnny Hodges ("Rabbit")
with some Chicago lettuce, 1958**

"…Coltrane got *The Times* obituary and Hodges didn't; that's the world we live in. Towards the end of his life Hodges' alto tone had become refined to the point at which it hardly seemed like an instrument: more like someone thinking. And, indeed, that's what it was."

Philip Larkin

© Terry Cryer

Freddie Green, London, 1959

"This is one of my favourite prints; added to which we talked of Lady Day."

Terry Cryer

© Terry Cryer

Paul Gonsalves at the Flamingo, Wardour Street; a private party for the Ellington Band, London, 1958

© Terry Cryer

Clara Ward, the gospel singer, at the 100 Club, London, 1959

© Terry Cryer

Phil Seaman at The Marquee, London, 1960

© Herman Leonard

Billie Holiday, New York, 1955

"While playing in the orchestra for *West Side Story*, Phil had a tendency to drop off during the gaps. One night during the performance, he awoke with a start, banging his elbow on the gong. He immediately stood up and declaimed, 'Dinner is served'."

Ronnie Scott

**Coleman Hawkins ("Bean"),
London, 1959**

"I don't think," he
says airily, "that I ever
was a child!"

Coleman Hawkins

© Mephisto

Duke Ellington and Bud Powell, Paris, 1960

In a November 1979 interview, Bill Evans told Norwegian jazz writer Randi Hultin: "If I had to choose one single musician for his artistic integrity, the incomparable originality of his creation and also the greatness of his work, it would be Bud Powell. Nobody can hold a candle to him."

"Never stand when you can sit down, never sit when you can lie down, and whatever you do don't cross your legs."

Duke Ellington (quote overheard)

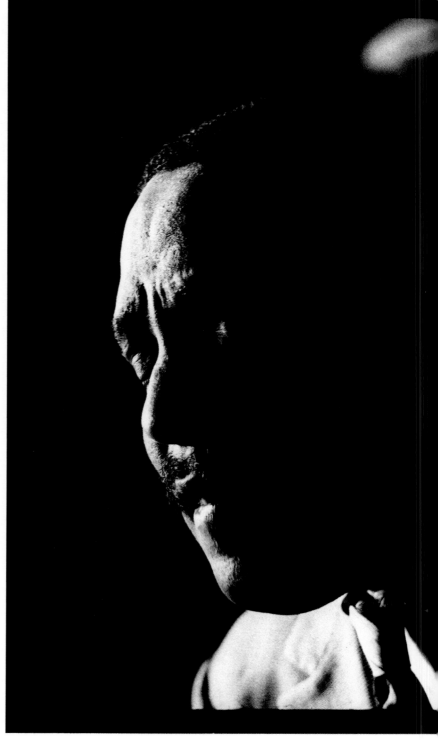

Bud Powell, Club St. Germain,
Paris, 1960

"Slam Stewart's bass solo, like all his solos, is bowed and hummed at the same time. But such gimmickry is only the surface; he sets up a constantly fanciful and varied continuity of riff figures, with great good humor."

Martin Williams

© Tim Motion

Slam Stewart, Alexandra Palace, 1979

© Jean-Pierre Leloir

Cootie Williams, Paris, 1963

Duke occasionally says, "Cootie gave the growl more beauty than anyone, more melodic magnificence. He had a sort of majestic folk quality. His open horn was wonderful – wonderful loud and wonderful soft. He had a hell of a style."

Richard O. Boyer

© David Redfern

Sonny Rollins, London, 1961

Duke Ellington and Billy Strayhorn, London, 1963

After a phone conversation to discuss a new composition: "Without really knowing it, I had a theme that was a kind of development of a similar theme he had written. So when he played my portion and went into his, it was as though we had really worked together – or one person had done it. It was an uncanny feeling, like witchcraft, like looking into someone else's mind."

Billy Strayhorn

© Jean-Pierre Leloir

Mahalia Jackson, the gospel singer, Hotel Georges V, Paris, 1961

"Playing with Miles, you might drop a bum chord in by mistake and he would resolve it in such a fine way."

Herbie Hancock

© Ray Avery

Miles Davis, Monterey, 1969

Charlie Mingus, Paris, 1964

"I heard this as a child when I went to meetings with my mother. The congregation gives their testimonial before the Lord, they confess their sins and sing and shout and do a little Holy Rolling. Some preachers cast out demons, they call their dialogue talking in tongues or talking unknown tongue (language the Devil can't understand)."

Charlie Mingus

Dizzy's valise

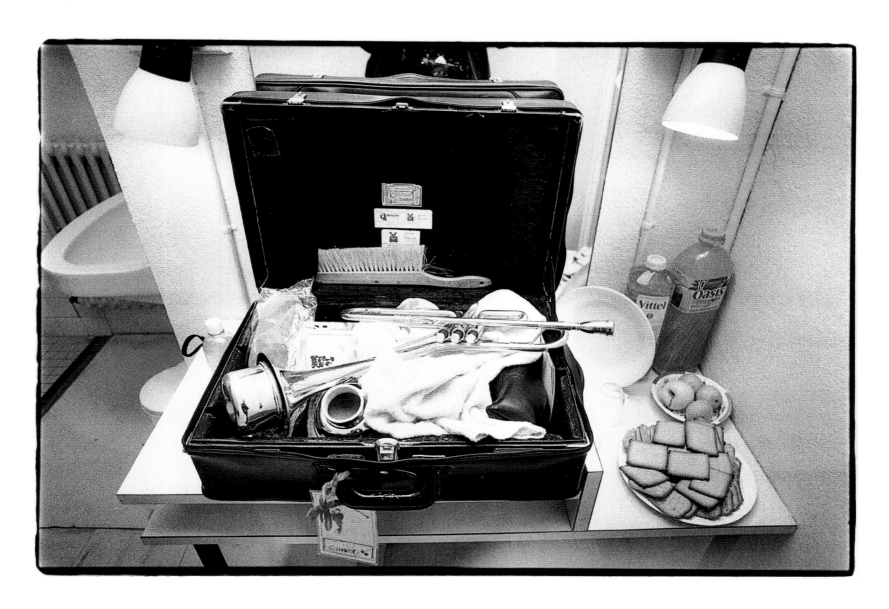

**John Lamb, Newport Jazz
Festival, 1966
(with the Duke Ellington Band)**

© Ray Avery

**Thelonious Sphere Monk,
Monterey, 1962**

"Coltrane, who played in one of the most inventive of Monk's groups in the '50s, said that if you missed a chord change it was 'like falling into an empty elevator shaft'."

John Fordham

© Francine Winham

John Coltrane, Newport, 1966

Jimmy Garrison, Ronnie Scott's "Old Place", London, 1957

Introducing a young Yugoslav pianist in his show 'Evolution of The Blues', Jon Hendricks said; "He's from Montenegro, so I guess he must be in there somewhere! "

"Jazzmobile" audience, Harlem, 1967

"Complete Communion. A neighbourhood audience on 119th Street applauds guitarist George Benson's group in the days when he still played jazz and before he became a household name. The occasion is one of the earliest Jazzmobile concerts, in which the music was taken back to the communities that had birthed it."

Val Wilmer

© Jean-Pierre Leloir

Archie Shepp, New York, 1969

"It is integral to my point of view that African-American music is the basis of the Negro's cultural experience here in the United States and that there are many social, political, and economical implications to this music."

Archie Shepp

© David Redfern

Ben Webster, London, 1970

© Jean-Pierre Leloir

Milt Jackson ("Bags"), Paris, 1970

© David Redfern

Stan Kenton, London, 1970

© Val Wilmer

**Rashied Ali and son Khalil, at
105-107 Broadway, Brooklyn, a
Williamsburg address well known
in the musicians' community.
Home to several noted
drummers; Coltrane used to
rehearse here.**

© Val Wilmer

**Jimmy Garrison at home,
New York, 1971**

Cecil Taylor backstage, New York, 1976

"Cecil Taylor believes (frankly, even bluntly, believes) that his music speaks for itself and that it should be allowed to."

Martin Williams

© Jak Kilby

Archie Shepp at The Roundhouse,
London, 1976

© Tim Motion

Bud Freeman and Vic Dickenson,
Alexandra Palace Jazz Festival,
1979

Overheard at a concert where Joe Newman
was playing, a woman in the audience leant
over to her friend and said: "That's the guy
that stole my cherry."

(quote overheard)

© Tim Motion

Budd Johnson, Alexandra Palace Jazz Festival, 1979

© Tim Motion

**Elvin Jones at Ronnie Scott's,
London, 1978**

"... Jones' fluid
rhythmic structures"

Max Harrison

Buck Clayton, Nice Jazz Festival, 1988

Stan Tracey, Ronnie Scott's, London, 1977

A pianist invited to sit in at Ronnie Scott's 'old place' where Stan Tracey was the regular pianist, was disconcerted to hear Stan whisper, indicating a couple of octaves on the keyboard: "From here to here, they don't work."

(quote overheard)

© Ray Avery

Chet Baker and the ghost of Bix:
Stars Of Jazz TV Show,
California, 1958

© Tim Motion

**Colin Smith and the ghost of
Duke: Pizza on the Park,
London, 1982**

**Herbie Hancock and Dizzy
Gillespie, Nice Jazz Festival,
1983**

© Carolina Benshemesh

**Stan Getz, Nice Jazz Festival,
1986**

© Tim Motion

**Stan Getz, Nice Jazz Festival,
1987**

Ronald Shannon Jackson, 1986

Lionel Hampton, Nice Jazz Festival, 1983

© Christian Him

'G'. Room at the Top, London,
1982

© Tim Motion

Chet Baker, The Canteen,
London, 1983

"I play every set as if
it were my last."

Chet Baker (quote to Christian Him)

Chris McGregor
of the Brotherhood of Breath,
London, 1987

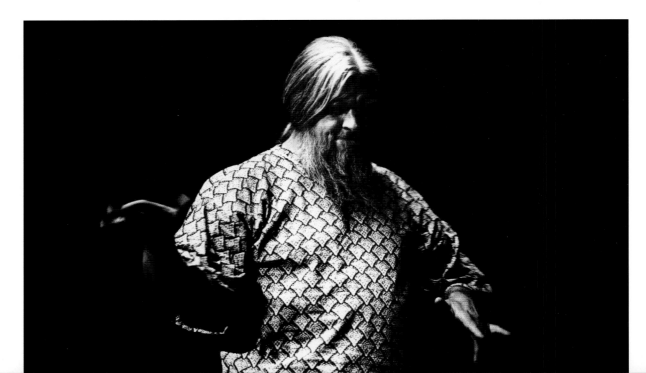

© Mephisto

Chris McGregor, Marne la Vallée, 1980

© Jak Kilby

**Sun Ra, with Marshall Allen and
John Gilmore, The Academy,
Brixton, London, 1984**

"... but then I heard some of his Saturn
arrangements and they were so beautiful.
His sound was so different from any sound
I ever heard."

John Gilmore

Sun Ra, Grafton Hotel,
London, 1991

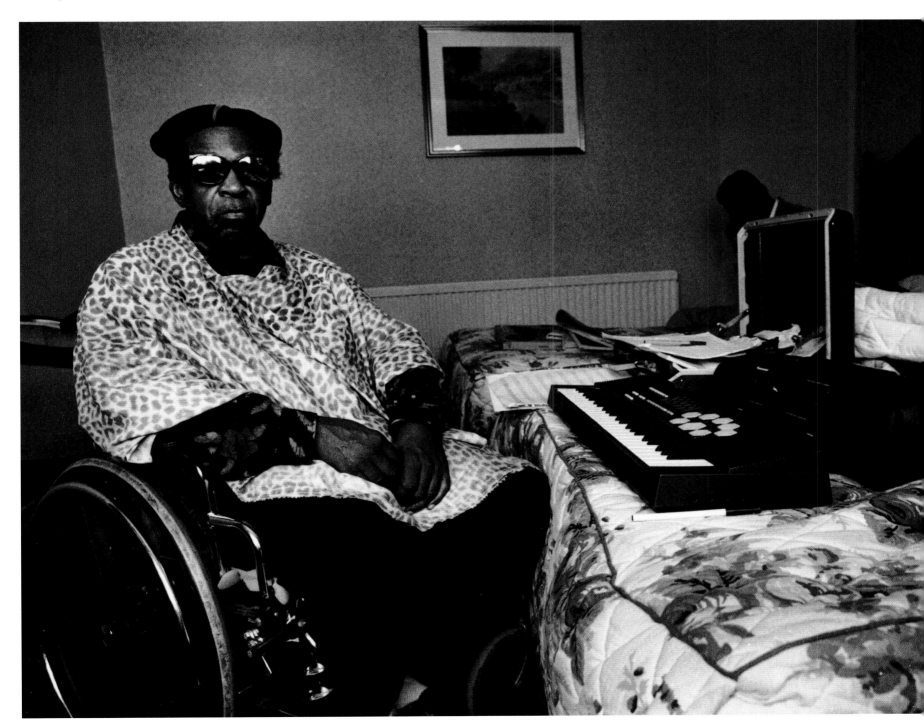

© Jak Kilby

Don Cherry, with Bob Stewart,
1993

"The naturalness of music is what I want to
be involved in. It's like the instruments playing
us, and I can really see now that it's time for
that because of the acoustic-ness and all the
instruments are working with overtones and
the idea is the swing in it and we're really
creating a nice boogie, you know."

Don Cherry

Dudu Pukwana, London, 1987

... of the Blue Notes with Louis Moholo, and Chris McGregor, Brotherhood of Breath.

© Peter Symes

Lester Bowie and Brass Fantasy,
Bath Festival, England, 1988

"I've been in this business for all these years, and if I can make as much money as my mailman, that's a good year for me. And *I'm* well known!"

Lester Bowie

"This wave, that wave... I feel now it's an all–wave music that's happening!"

Don Cherry

© Val Wilmer

Billy Bang, lower east side Manhattan, 1986

A prominent member of what can best be described as the Third Wave of "free jazz" musicians.

© Tim Motion

Dizzy Gillespie, Nice Jazz
Festival, 1986

There was a pertinent epitaph for Dizzy Gillespie by E.J. Thribb (17½) in *Private Eye* which went like this:
"So. Farewell
Then
Dizzy Gillespie
Famous jazz
Trumpeter
You were well known
For your
Bulging cheeks.
Rudolph Nureyev.
So were
You."

Although I am tired of the commercialization of Dizzy's cheeks and his 'funny horn', and forbade other photographers to submit such pictures for this book, I like this image and include it in the vain hope that it may be the last 'word' on the matter, and that people will listen to his brilliant music.

Meanwhile I would like to quote in full the one column entry for "Ragtime and Jazz" in the 1952 edition of *The Concise Oxford Dictionary of Music* by Percy A. Scholes:

"Ragtime is a type of music of Amer. negro origin, in which the classic rhythmic device of syncopation (q.v.) is carried to an extreme. It has been known since at least as early as 1880 but the wider Amer. world and the European world first became aware of it about 1911, when Irving Berlin's 'Alexander's Ragtime Band' was publ. The use of a great variety of noisy percussion instruments, and other instruments played in new ways (e.g. the trumpet played with blatant tone and the trombone played with *glissando*), became characteristics: the most distinctive instrument used has been the saxophone. The name 'Jazz' soon tended to supersede 'Ragtime'. Primarily 'Ragtime' and 'Jazz' were and are dance music manifestations, but they have made appearances in the concert room under such descriptions as 'Symphonised Syncopation'. Other names have, from time to time, been given to this order of music or some of its phases – e.g. 'Swing Music' and (strange attempt at a monopoly application of an ancient and general term!) 'Rhythm Music'. Adepts and addicts make distinctions in their application of such terms, but these distinctions are difficult to understand and seem sometimes to be contradictory of one another.

An element of extemporization has throughout been a feature of music of this kind as performed by the more accomplished bands of players, in which individuals enjoy liberty melodically to embellish their parts, as also to fill in gaps between the ending of one section and the beginning of another by what are called 'breaks' (it is understood that 'Straight Jazz' implies adherence to the composer's score and 'Hot Jazz' a free use of the improvisatory element): sometimes the performers burst into vocal utterance."

I am glad to say that later editions have been extensively expanded and revised.

Emily Remler, Nice Jazz Festival, 1986

"But there's still a lot of things that bother me. Like people worrying about your looks when all you want to think about is the music."

Emily Remler

Emily Remler died, reportedly of a heart attack, in Sydney, Australia, in 1990. She was thirty-two years old.

Double-bass scroll.
London Jazz Festival, 1993

© Andrew Pothecary

**Andrew Hill, Queen Elizabeth
Hall, London, 1991**

"He [Charlie Parker] was telling me there was a time in my life when I will be a keeper of the flame, simply from having experienced certain areas of music in the black tradition, things that only I and a few others really know about."

Andrew Hill

© Peter Symes

Andy Shepherd, "sound check",
Festival Hall, London, 1990

McCoy Tyner, pianist and integral part of the original Coltrane Quartet, was playing at a jazz festival in Japan recently and noticed, in front of the audience, a group of people kneeling in an attitude of prayer. After the performance he spoke with them and asked them why they had been praying. They replied, "Tyner-san, mourning Coltrane."

(quote from Orphy Robinson)

© Mephisto

Carla Bley and Andy Shepherd,
Le Mans, France, 1994

**Paul Burwell, Institute of
Contemporary Arts, London, 1992**

"White drummer – black paint."

© Jak Kilby

Stan Tracey, Ronnie Scott's,
London, 1994

(To the piano)
"Hello, old adversary."

Stan Tracey

Stan Tracey, on being
asked what his secret
was, replied, "Celibacy
and Mars Bars."

(quote to David Sinclair)

© Tim Motion

Elaine Delmar, jazz singer,
London, 1980

Annie Whitehead, London, 1993

© Jennifer Sebley

**Lol Coxhill, at the Tate Gallery,
London, 1994**

© David Sinclair

**Lol Coxhill, Queen Elizabeth Hall,
London, 1993**

**Don't call it new
Don't call it old
Out/in, avant/derrière
Don't chain it with 'freedom'
or insist that it be 'ethnic'**

**Don't categorize, conceptualize,
   hypothesize or listen with your
   eyes,
Don't worry if it's up, down, front,
back, "swing", "rock", "blues",
"bop", "classical" or even "art".**

**Study the history and
   acknowledge the source
But remember, it all comes
   from the heart and
Please Please Please**

Listen

poem: Ray Anderson

© Jonathan Oppong-Wiafe

Wayne Batchelor, London, 1993

Delfeayo Marsalis, London, 1993

© Tim Motion

Charlie Haden,
Nice Jazz Festival, 1984

Appropriately for the leader of the
1969 Liberation Music Orchestra,
this shot was taken on Bastille
Day, July 14th.

"People have lost their appreciation for beauty. The great thing about this art form is that musicians care about beautiful sound. They want to make their instruments sound really beautiful."

Charlie Haden

Nana Vasconcelos, **Queen**
Elizabeth Hall, **London**, **1991**

"...[his] myriad approaches to rhythm utilize shakers, drums, berimbau (a bow tapped with a stick), and body percussion."
W. Royal Stokes

© David Redfern

Claire Martin, jazz singer,
London, 1992

© Christian Him

Stephane Grappelli, The Barbican, London, 1993, at his eighty-fifth birthday celebration.

© Chris Windsor

Nikki Yeou, Jazz Café, London, 1994

"Her belief in the ubiquity of music is deeply rooted and profound."

Eddie Brannan

© Chris Windsor

Pharoah Sanders, London, 1994

© David Sinclair

**Michel Petrucciani, Royal
Festival Hall, London, 1994**

© Danny Ferri

**Abe Laboriel, Montreux Jazz
Festival, 1992**

© Tim Motion

Dee Dee Bridgewater,
'Jazz à Juan' 1989, Antibes,
France

**Miles Davis, New Orleans Jazz
and Heritage Festival, 1986**

No liner notes, Miles
said. "There's nothing
to say about the
music," he told
Ralph J Gleason.
"Don't write about
the music. The music
speaks for itself."

Miles Davis

© Danny Ferri

**Gospel Singer, Montreux Jazz
Festival, 1992**

© Danny Ferri

**Steve Ferrone, drummer with
Milt Jackson, Montreux Jazz
Festival, 1992**

© Jak Kilby

Art and Akira Blakey,

"Every time we find a youngster, we work on him. And then he finds out for himself."

'Old Man' Jo Jones, drummer

© Tim Motion

Abdullah Ibn Buhaina

Art Blakey, London, 1979

"He'd make you play. By the time he gets through kicking you in the ass, if you don't get up and play something, you sound like you're a weakling."

Horace Silver

index of artists

acknowledgements

I wish to express my gratitude to all jazz musicians for their inspiring music, which makes possible the images reproduced in this book, and especially to two good friends no longer with us, Art Blakey and Oliver Jackson.

Thanks to Will Steeds, previous editor at Salamander, for giving the idea a kick-start, and to Richard Collins, Rachel Boone and Paul Johnson at Salamander for their positive help and patience in preparing the material for publication.

Thanks also to Lucie, David and Paul Motion for their help and affirmation, in operating the computer and word processor, explaining mysteries and typing text; and to Fabian Jolivet in Los Angeles, Laura Watts in Birmingham and Jonathan Abbott in London for contacts and promotion work propagating the jazz image, and Angus James, Peter Ind and Michael Horovitz,

for the loan of ears and books.

Finally, thanks to the twenty-three photographers who submitted their work, for their fine photographs, co-operation and enthusiasm, Peter Boizot and the Pizza Express jazz venture, and to Ronnie Scott and Pete King for managing to keep the club open for thirty-five years as somewhere to go at night.

Tim Motion

QUOTES

Page 5: poem by Michael Horovitz, London 1979, from 'Growing Up: Selected Poems and Pictures' 1951-79, Allison & Busby; 14: Ralph J Gleason, Down Beat, 1952; 16: (top) The Encyclopedia of Jazz, Salamander Books, 1978; (bottom) New Orleans Music, Vol. 1 No.1, 1989; 18, 20, 34, 48: Jazz Anecdotes, Bill Crow, 1990; 22: Bird: The Legend of Charlie Parker, Robert Reisner, Quartet Books; 23: sleeve notes for Manhattan Symphonie, Dexter Gordon Quartet,

CBS 1978; 24, 26, 27, 66, 94, 96, 97, 101, 103, 115: The Jazz Scene, Oxford University Press, 1991; 36: New Departures No. 4, 1963; 37: interview with Kevin Whitehead, Down Beat, 1995; 40: (centre) Dave Dexter Jr., Hindsight Records, 1986; 42: 'All What Jazz', from The Jazz Anthology, Miles Kington, Harper Collins, 1993; 49: Mike Hennessy, 'Dancing With Infidels', Jazz on CD magazine, 1995; 53, 72: Jazz Heritage, Oxford University Press New York; 54: 'The Hot Bach' (1944), from The Duke Ellington Reader, Oxford University Press New York; 56: from 1962 Coss interview, ibid.; 59: from his album 'Blues and Roots, Atlantic Records; 63: JAZZ, Dorling Kindersley; 76: A Jazz Retrospect, Quartet Books; 92: from an interview with David Block, Jazz Journal, 1994; 98: Private Eye magazine, London; 111: JAZZ: A History, Frank Tirro, W W Norton & Co., Inc., 1993; 114: 'Waiting For

Dizzy', Gene Lees, 1991, Oxford University Press New York; 118: Jazz on CD magazine, 1995; 'Miles Davis – Dig', Doug Ramsey, from The Jazz Anthology, Miles Kington, Harper Collins, 1993; 126: (top) The Face of Black Music, Val Wilmer, Da Capo Press, Inc.; (bottom) Jazz Times, 1994.

PHOTO CREDITS

Endpapers: Courtney Pine, 1992, by Francine Winham; page 2: Al Grey, by Tim Motion; 4: Charlie 'Bird' Parker, by Tim Motion, 1968, painted in Portugal from an obscure photograph, while listening to the Massey Hall Concert; 6: Ronnie Scott at Bletchingley Village Hall, Surrey, 1989, by David Sinclair; 11: Herman Leonard by Danny Ferri; Tim Motion and David Redfern by Linda Rosier; Andrew Pothecary by Jane Wexler; Francine Winham by Dee Dee Glass; 81: Duke Ellington poster in background by David Redfern.